DiscoverRoo
An Imprint of Pop!
popbooksonline.com

Creatures of Legend

# WENDIGO

## FIRST NATION'S FOREST FEASTER

by Elizabeth Andrews

abdobooks.com

Published by Pop!, a division of ABDO, PO Box 398166, Minneapolis, Minnesota 55439. 

Printed in the United States of America, North Mankato, Minnesota.

052022
092022

THIS BOOK CONTAINS RECYCLED MATERIALS

Cover Photo: Shutterstock Images

Interior Photos: Shutterstock Images, Historia/Shutterstock, Universal History Archive/Shutterstock, Moviestore/Shutterstock, Roland W. Reed, George M. Dawson/Library and Archives Canada

Editor: Bridget O'Brien
Series Designer: Laura Graphenteen

**Library of Congress Control Number: 2021951842**

**Publisher's Cataloging-in-Publication Data**

Names: Andrews, Elizabeth, author.

Title: Wendigo: First Nation's forest feaster / by Elizabeth Andrews

Other title: First Nation's forest feaster

Description: Minneapolis, Minnesota : Pop, 2023 | Series: Creatures of legend | Includes online resources and index

Identifiers: ISBN 9781098242381 (lib. bdg.) | ISBN 9781098243081 (ebook)

Subjects: LCSH: Windigos--Juvenile literature. | Monsters--Juvenile literature. | Animals--Folklore--Juvenile literature. | Fabled creatures--Juvenile literature.

Classification: DDC 001.944--dc23

# WELCOME TO DiscoverRoo!

Pop open this book and you'll find QR codes loaded with information, so you can learn even more!

Scan this code* and others like it while you read, or visit the website below to make this book pop!

**popbooksonline.com/wendigo**

*Scanning QR codes requires a web-enabled smart device with a QR code reader app and a camera.

# TABLE OF CONTENTS

CHAPTER 1

# LEGENDS TO TELL IN THE DARK

In the cold, dark woods of northern Minnesota, a family sits around a crackling campfire. A young boy waits patiently for his uncle to start speaking. The uncle begins a frightening tale about a Wendigo that haunts the woods when the weather gets cold.

WATCH A VIDEO HERE!

*There are endless scary legends to share around a campfire.*

*The coldest temperature recorded in Minnesota was -60°F (-51°C).*

Hundreds of years ago the Wendigo was once a man, just like the people sitting around the fire that night. It wandered the very woods the family visits today. It felt love, anger, and fear like any human. Trouble arose when a particularly freezing winter hit.

**DID YOU KNOW?**

Wendigo is also spelled "Windigo," "Wiindigoo," and even "Wittika."

*Keeping a fire going during a camping trip can protect against dangerous creatures.*

The young boy listens to this important story. The tale has been told for countless generations. He learns what happens when a human makes the monstrous choice that turns a heart to ice. This choice will turn man to monster.

*Once a Wendigo starts hunting a person, there is no hope of survival.*

CHAPTER 2

# ALGONQUIAN PEOPLES AND THEIR MYTHS

The Wendigo myth began among Algonquian-speaking peoples. These peoples were **indigenous** to North America. They called the land home before any European person arrived.

EXPLORE LINKS HERE!

# WHERE WAS THE LEGEND TOLD?

Wendigo tales are told by Algonquian-speaking tribes. They live in forests of the Great Lakes and through Canada's central and east coast regions. Many different indigenous tribes historically occupied this land. They included Cree, Ojibwe, Ottawa, Algonquin, and Potawatomi.

*Some Lake Superior Ojibwe were the first to live on the Apostle Islands of Wisconsin.*

Myths and legends are often passed down **orally** in indigenous communities. The stories are important connections between people living today and their **ancestors**. There are usually moral lessons woven into the legends.

The Wendigo's lesson is about **greed** and **gluttony**. It is also a warning about the true power of winter.

Wendigos are not born. They are made. A human must commit the worst of sins and eat human flesh to turn into a Wendigo. People do not seek out the change. It usually happens at a point of desperate starvation in the winter.

**DID YOU KNOW?**

The first Wendigo might have been a female warrior who drank the blood of her enemies to gain extra strength and defeat them in battle.

*Indigenous people made birch bark canoes.*

Hundreds of years ago, winter was a life-threatening time. There were no grocery stores for food supplies or furnaces pumping warm air into homes. People had to prepare beforehand.

*Indigenous people often wore two layers of fur clothing during the cold winter months.*

*Some winter tents can have stoves inside. This helps people stay warm.*

Sometimes, all the preparation in the world could not keep a person safe in winter. In those years, people often died of starvation or exposure. It was during these hard winters that people might have made the horrible decision to kill and eat another human for survival.

*Members of the Ojibwe tribe were fur traders around the Great Lakes.*

CHAPTER 3

# HEARTS OF ICE

Wendigos don't look the same from story to story. Each tribe has its own version. Sometimes they were giants. These Wendigos would run across treetops hunting their next meal. Other times, the Wendigo was the size of a human.

LEARN MORE HERE!

**DID YOU KNOW?**

The original Algonquian legend did not describe horned Wendigos. Popular culture changed the true myth.

The two monsters had similarities. A Wendigo's lips are eaten away to show yellow fangs. It was as though the monster was so hungry for human flesh

*Giant Wendigos move very quickly.*

that it ate its own. No matter the body size, the Wendigo's bones poke through its skin. The eyes lie deep in its head. And it always smells of death.

Wendigos have an unending hunger for human flesh. It makes them good hunters. They must be when stalking prey as smart as humans. Wendigos have the power to bring about sudden snowstorms. The humans they hunt will get confused and lost in the woods, a very **vulnerable** place for a person to be.

There is one truth to all Wendigos: their hearts are solid ice. This is the magic of the Wendigo spirit. Once a human makes the decision to consume the flesh of another, the Wendigo spirit takes over and the shift begins. **Indigenous** legends spoke of people dreaming

## WENDIGO CURE

**Legend says that there is a cure for humans turned Wendigo. After they ate human flesh, their hearts froze. Wendigos would be held down next to a strong fire to start the warming process. Then, boiling hot animal fat would be poured down their throat. The goal of the cure was to thaw the heart from the inside.**

*A person with a frozen heart has lost all their humanity.*

about eating humans. These dreams were taken very seriously. The person who had the dream would ask for help from a tribe healer. The dreamer would be watched and cared for to prevent completing the Wendigo transformation.

CHAPTER 4

# MODERN WENDIGO

As the centuries passed, written documentation of Wendigos became more common. In the late 1800s, many cases of people who turned into Wendigos sparked public interest.

The most famous was a man named Swift Runner from the Cree tribe of

COMPLETE AN ACTIVITY HERE!

Alberta, Canada. Swift Runner was very popular with his tribe. But he fell onto hard times and was sent away with his family when he started showing signs of violence. The first winter in exile was hard. Swift Runner lost his whole family.

*Swift Runner was arrested in Canada.*

When his old tribe saw Swift Runner after the hard winter, he was in good physical shape. This was suspicious. The tribe became concerned when Swift Runner was caught trying to lure children into the woods. Police went to his camp and found evidence that he had eaten his family. Swift Runner was a Wendigo. He was arrested.

Swift Runner was not the only person to be arrested for crimes committed as a Wendigo around that time. People said they had committed murders because

*The people claiming to be possessed by Wendigo spirits did not have physical changes.*

they were **possessed** by a Wendigo spirit. Some also claimed to have killed a person to prevent them from becoming a Wendigo. The late 1800s were so busy with Wendigo-related crimes that the time became known as the Wendigo Trials.

**DID YOU KNOW?** Marvel Comics has stories that feature horned Wendigo creatures.

The Wendigo tale is special because of its rich history passed between Algonquian speakers. Unfortunately, popular culture in the modern world has dramatically changed the **indigenous** story.

Famous author Stephen King wrote about a big, ugly, horned monster called the Wendigo in his novel *Pet Semetery*. This description spread and is now how most people picture the Wendigo. It no longer gets paired with the original lesson of **greed** and **gluttony** that was the indigenous story's purpose.

*Pet Cemetery was made into a movie.*

# MAKING CONNECTIONS

## TEXT-TO-SELF

Have you ever spent time in the woods during winter? What do you imagine it would feel like living there?

## TEXT-TO-TEXT

Have you read any other books about indigenous legends? What did they have in common with the Wendigo legend?

## TEXT-TO-WORLD

Do you think it is okay for popular culture to change original legends? Please explain your answer.

# GLOSSARY

**ancestor** — a family member who lived several generations ago.

**gluttony** — the habit or an instance of excessive eating and drinking.

**greed** — a great desire for more than what someone needs or deserves.

**indigenous** — the earliest known inhabitants of a place; of or having to do with people or animals that originally lived and may continue to live in a particular country or region.

**oral** — spoken, rather than written.

**possess** — to take control of something or someone.

**vulnerable** — open to attack or danger.

# INDEX



# ONLINE RESOURCES

## popbooksonline.com

Scan this code* and others like it while you read, or visit the website below to make this book pop!

**popbooksonline.com/wendigo**

*Scanning QR codes requires a web-enabled smart device with a QR code reader app and a camera.